THE BATTLE OF
THE BULGE

TURNING BACK HITLER'S FINAL PUSH

By **Bill Cain** Illustrated by **Dheeraj Verma**

New York

Published in 2008 by The Rosen Publishing Group, Inc.
29 East 21st Street, New York, NY 10010

First edition, 2008

Photo Credits:
pp. 4, 5, 7, 44, 45 National Archives and Records Administration; p. 6 Courtesy of the Department of Defense.

Library of Congress Cataloging-in-Publication Data

Cain, Bill.
The Battle of the Bulge : turning back Hitler's final push / by Bill Cain ; illustrated by Dheeraj Verma.
p. cm. -- (Graphic battles of World War II)
Includes index.
ISBN-13: 978-1-4042-0782-0(library binding)   978-1-4042-7422-8(pbk.)
6-pack ISBN-13: 978-1-4042-7423-5

1. Ardennes, Battle of the, 1944–1945. I. Verma, Dheeraj. II. Title.
D756.5.A7C34 2008
940.54'219348--dc22
                    2007026862

CONTENTS

WORLD WAR II, 1939–1945

Even after World War I (1914–1918), there were strong hostilities between many nations. The United States worked to build good relations with other countries to avoid fighting another war.

However, other nations were becoming aggressive toward their neighbors. In 1936, Italy invaded Ethiopia. Japan attacked China in 1937. In 1938, Germany took control of Austria and Czechoslovakia.

In 1939, Germany invaded Poland. France and England responded by declaring war on Germany. The United States had avoided fighting in the growing worldwide conflict, but on December 7, 1941, Japan attacked the U.S. naval base at Pearl Harbor, Hawaii. America was at war.

For the next four years, the United States and its allies fought Germany and its allies on land, on the sea, and in the air. One of the most brutal battles was fought at the Battle of the Bulge, between December 1944 and January 1945.

KEY COMMANDERS

Lieutenant General Omar Bradley
was senior U.S. field commander and in charge of the Twelfth Army Group. He was known for his great management and tactical skills.

Lieutenant General George S. Patton
was in charge of the Third Army, part of Bradley's Twelfth Army Group. His intelligence team (G-2) warned the Allies of the German offensive in the Ardennes.

SS Oberstgruppenfuehrer Josef "Sepp" Dietrich
was commander of the 6th Panzer Army at the Battle of the Bulge. Dietrich was very popular with his men.

General der Panzertruppe Hasso von Manteuffel
was commander of the 5th Panzer Army at the battle. He was, however, also a personal favorite of Adolf Hitler's.

3

D-DAY AND BEYOND

The Battle of the Bulge (also known as the Battle of the Ardennes) was one of the bloodiest and most important campaigns of the Second World War, a last great effort by the Germans to defeat the western Allies before their armies reached Germany itself. Code named *Wacht am Rhein* ("Watch on the Rhine"), the German offensive was planned in complete secrecy, and when it was launched on December 16, 1944, the Allies were taken completely by surprise. If the Germans had won, they might have captured the vital port of Antwerp, split the Allies in two, and forced them to negotiate a peace treaty. However, the dense forests, hilly ground, and winter weather that hid the German buildup would eventually work in favor of the Allies.

When the British, the Americans, and the Canadians landed on the beaches of Normandy on June 6, 1944, they managed to fight their way ashore and carve out a small beachhead. In the months that followed, the Allies made several attempts to push inland, but the

Adolf Hitler (center) dominated all German military planning. It was he who decided on the Ardennes offensive.

outnumbered Germans fought a skillful defensive campaign, forcing the Allies to pay heavily for every yard of ground. However, in August 1944, the thinly held German line cracked under the pressure, and the Allies were able to surround and destroy the bulk of the German army in the "Falaise Pocket." This operation was known as the "breakout from Normandy." As the German survivors retreated, the Allies spread out across France, liberating Paris and driving on into Belgium to the north and the French provinces of Alsace and Lorraine in the east.

The biggest problem facing the Allies was getting food, fuel, and ammunition to the troops spearheading the Allied advance. All their supplies had to be transported from Normandy, and soon the Allied advance began to slow down because of a lack of fuel. The capture of the port of Antwerp in Belgium should have eased the problem. However, small German pockets still held out in the area, and it wasn't until the start of December that the first supplies could be landed there. Meanwhile, the Germans had managed to regroup and form a defensive line along the border of Belgium and Holland as well as in Alsace-Lorraine, stretching south from Luxembourg to the border of Switzerland.

Taken by an anonymous German military cameraman, this photo shows the Germans advancing to form their defensive line.

On September 17, the British field marshal Bernard Montgomery launched Operation Market Garden. This involved the dropping of parachute divisions along the Allied line of advance, capturing the bridges needed for the rest of the army to cross the River Rhine, and pushing into Germany. Unfortunately the Germans were able to overrun the British 1st Airborne Division at Arnhem before the rest of the Allied army could rescue them. The operation succeeded in liberating most of southern Holland, but the disaster at Arnhem meant that the Germans were able to stop the Allies before they reached German soil.

As the British became bogged down in Holland, Lieutenant General George S. Patton's U.S. Third Army was fighting a grueling campaign in Alsace-Lorraine, an area where the Germans had built their West Wall, a belt of fortifications that slowed the American advance to a crawl. Between Patton

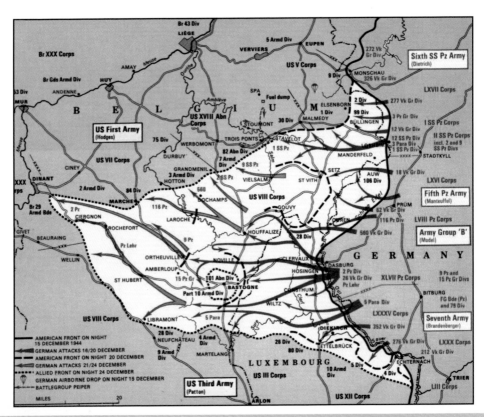

The Battle of the Bulge took place in Belgium and Luxembourg, with the Belgian towns of Bastogne and St. Vith the centers of most of the action. Surprised by a large German Panzer force, U.S. forces struggled for ten days to fight off the attack.

The Belgian landscape of snowy fields, hills, and forest meant many soliders were exposed during the battle.

and Montgomery lay the Ardennes—an area of dense forests and small winding roads that the Allies thought was unsuitable for offensive operations. Farther to the north were the city of Aachen and the Hürtgen Forest, where General Courtney Hodges's U.S. First Army became embroiled in another bloody battle. Hodges used the quiet sector of the Ardennes as a place where his battered American divisions could rest and recover.

None of these soldiers suspected that a few miles to the east the Germans were secretly building up a powerful army group and preparing to launch it through the Ardennes toward the coast. The Allies failed to detect this German buildup, and by mid-December everything was ready. Three German armies would take part in *Wacht am Rhein*. To the north, the 6th Panzer Army would spearhead the drive on Antwerp, supported to the south by the 5th Panzer Army, which would capture the strategic Ardennes town of Bastogne, then drive on to the Meuse River. To the south, the smaller 7th Army would protect the southern flank of the German offensive against

Patton's U.S. Third Army. In all, some thirty German divisions were involved in the attack—a third of a million men.

Success for the Germans depended on three things. First, the attack had to be a complete surprise. Second, they needed bad weather to keep the Allied aircraft on the ground. Third, the Germans were desperately short of fuel, so they needed to capture as much fuel as they could from the Allies as they advanced. It was all a great gamble—Germany's last chance to defeat the Allies and end the war before Germany itself became a battleground.

Many U.S. soldiers huddled in ditches and snow drifts during the battle, trying to survive both the conditions and the enemy.

THE BATTLE OF THE BULGE
TURNING BACK HITLER'S FINAL PUSH

WINTER, 1944. THE GERMANS ARE RETREATING FROM THE RUSSIAN EASTERN FRONT IN TOTAL DEFEAT.

AFTER THE ALLIES GROUNDED THE GERMAN AIR FORCE, OR LUFTWAFFE, THE GERMANS HAD NO WAY TO GATHER INTELLIGENCE OR STOP THE ALLIED ADVANCE IN THE SOUTH AND WEST.

THE GERMANS ARE FIGHTING A DEFENSIVE CAMPAIGN AND CAN'T DO MAJOR OFFENSIVE OPERATIONS.

BRITISH FIELD MARSHAL BERNARD MONTGOMERY, COMMANDER OF THE 21ST ARMY GROUP.

GERMAN LEADER ADOLF HITLER SEARCHED FOR A WAY TO HALT THE ALLIED ADVANCE AND REGAIN THE UPPER HAND IN THE WAR.

THE ALLIES ARE OVERCONFIDENT. DESPITE WHAT MY INFERIORS MAY THINK, THEY MUST BE TAUGHT THAT GERMANY WILL *NEVER* SURRENDER!

THINGS LOOKED GOOD FOR THE ALLIES. FRESH FROM HUGE VICTORIES IN NORMANDY . . .

. . . AND LANDINGS IN SOUTHERN FRANCE, THE ALLIES ADVANCED TOWARD BERLIN, GERMANY, FASTER THAN ANYONE EXPECTED, TO FINISH OFF THE LAST OF THE GERMAN ARMY.

MERCI, MON AMI!*

*THANK YOU, MY FRIEND.

HITLER PLANNED A DARING ATTACK CALLED "WATCH ON THE RHINE" TO SPLIT THE ALLIES AND REGAIN CONTROL OF GERMANY'S WESTERN FRONT.

ANTWERP

SOON YOU WILL SEE COLLAPSE AND PANIC AMONG THE AMERICANS!

HITLER PLANNED TO QUICKLY CROSS THE MEUSE RIVER AND TAKE CONTROL OF THE BELGIAN PORT OF ANTWERP. ANTWERP WAS A VITAL SUPPLY ROUTE.

HIS PLAN RELIED ON FOUR ELEMENTS: SPEED, SURPRISE, BAD WEATHER TO KEEP ALLIED PLANES ON THE GROUND, AND CAPTURING ALLIED FUEL.

THE GERMANS PASSED ON PLANS VIA TELEGRAPH AND TELEPHONE, ROBBING THE ALLIES OF THEIR MOST POWERFUL WEAPON: ULTRA INTERCEPTS.*

*THE SYSTEM USED BY BRITISH AND AMERICAN INTELLIGENCE TO DECODE SECRET GERMAN MESSAGES.

JUST LIKE HIS EARLY SUCCESSES IN EUROPE IN 1940, HITLER WAS CONVINCED VICTORY WOULD BE HIS AGAIN.

ES BRAUST EIN RUF WIE DONNERHALL, WIE SCHWERTGEKLIRR UND WOGENPRALL*

"WATCH ON THE RHINE" WOULD BECOME MORE THAN JUST THE NAME OF A PATRIOTIC SONG . . . IT WOULD GIVE NEW LIFE TO THE THIRD REICH!

*TRANSLATION: "A CALL ROARS LIKE THUNDERBOLT, LIKE CLASHING SWORDS AND SPLASHING WAVES."

THE GERMANS MOVED 200,000 TROOPS WITH 500 TANKS INTO THE ARDENNES FOREST TO ATTACK ALONG THREE ROUTES INTO ALLIED POSITIONS.

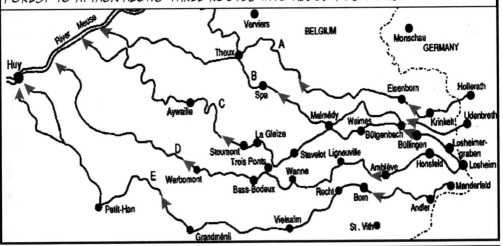

LEADING THE ATTACK WOULD BE LEGENDARY SS GENERAL SEPP DIETRICH. HIS MISSION WOULD BE TO SEIZE THE IMPORTANT PORT OF ANTWERP, BELGIUM.

GENERAL HASSO VON MANTEUFFEL'S 5TH PANZER ARMY WOULD ATTACK IN THE MIDDLE AND TRY TO CAPTURE THE TOWN OF BRUSSELS.

THE SOUTHERNMOST ATTACK BY THE FIFTEENTH ARMY WAS DESIGNED TO KEEP THE ALLIES IN PLACE AND SUPPORT THE OTHER TWO ATTACK ROUTES.

DECEMBER 16, 1944. THE BATTLE BEGAN BEFORE SUNRISE WITH A HUGE ARTILLERY ATTACK.

FIRE!

BOOM

SOLDIERS FROM NEWLY ARRIVED UNITS LIKE THE 106TH INFANTRY DIVISION WONDERED WHAT WAS GOING ON IN THE USUALLY QUIET WOODS.

HEY! DO YOU SEE THAT? IS THAT FIREWORKS?

ACROSS THE 80-MILE FRONT, 2,000 GERMAN ARTILLERY HOWITZERS BEGAN SPITTING FIRE AND LAUNCHING A RAIN OF STEEL DEATH ON THE LIGHTLY DEFENDED ALLIED LINE.

AAARGH!

OPERATION "WATCH ON THE RHINE" HAD BEGUN.

THE U.S. 99TH INFANTRY DIVISION, A NEWLY ARRIVED UNIT WITH NO COMBAT EXPERIENCE, WAS ALSO UNDER HEAVY ATTACK.

HOW CAN WE WIN AGAINST THESE GUYS? THEY'VE BEEN DOING THIS FOR YEARS!

THE INEXPERIENCED "BATTLE BABIES" FOUND THEMSELVES ALONE WHILE THE WEHRMACHT'S BEST TROOPS ATTACKED THEIR THINLY HELD LINE.

AAARGH!

THE 99TH COMMANDER, MAJOR GENERAL LAUER, ORDERED HIS SOLDIERS TO HOLD THE LINE.

HIT BACK WITH EVERYTHING WE'VE GOT! UNTIL WE KNOW WHAT'S GOING ON AROUND US, DON'T GIVE AN INCH!

THE ORDERS, PASSED TO EACH GERMAN UNIT, WERE VERY CLEAR . . .

SOLDIERS OF THE WEST FRONT: YOUR GREAT HOUR HAS STRUCK. EVERYTHING IS AT STAKE. YOU BEAR A HOLY DUTY TO ACHIEVE THE SUPERHUMAN FOR OUR FUEHRER!

HESSEN IS IN CENTRAL GERMANY, EAST OF WHERE THE FIGHTING WAS TAKING PLACE.

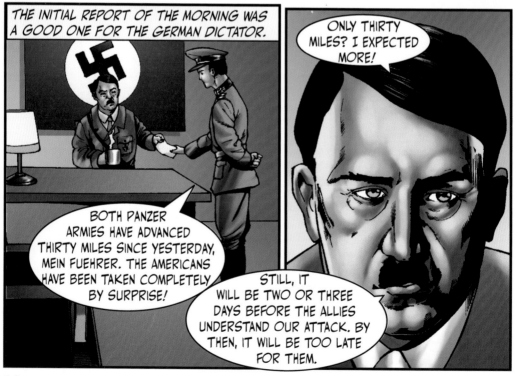

THE INITIAL REPORT OF THE MORNING WAS A GOOD ONE FOR THE GERMAN DICTATOR.

ONLY THIRTY MILES? I EXPECTED MORE!

BOTH PANZER ARMIES HAVE ADVANCED THIRTY MILES SINCE YESTERDAY, MEIN FUEHRER. THE AMERICANS HAVE BEEN TAKEN COMPLETELY BY SURPRISE!

STILL, IT WILL BE TWO OR THREE DAYS BEFORE THE ALLIES UNDERSTAND OUR ATTACK. BY THEN, IT WILL BE TOO LATE FOR THEM.

FROM HIS HEADQUARTERS IN VERSAILLES, FRANCE, GENERAL EISENHOWER MET WITH GENERAL OMAR BRADLEY, 12TH ARMY GROUP COMMANDER.

WE ARE GETTING REPORTS OF SMALL ATTACKS ACROSS THE FRONT, BUT THIS IS MOST LIKELY NOTHING IMPORTANT, SIR.

THAT SEEMS TO BE THE CONVENTIONAL WISDOM, BRAD. BUT I THINK HITLER'S TRYING SOMETHING VERY BIG.

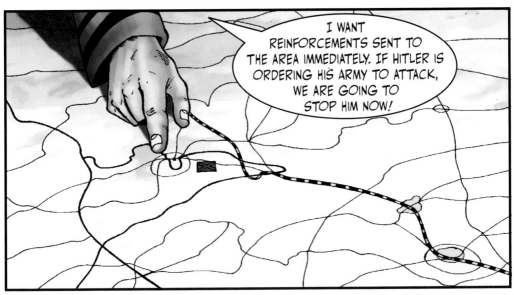

I WANT REINFORCEMENTS SENT TO THE AREA IMMEDIATELY. IF HITLER IS ORDERING HIS ARMY TO ATTACK, WE ARE GOING TO STOP HIM NOW!

A MAJOR PART OF "WATCH ON THE RHINE" WAS AN AIRBORNE ATTACK BY 1,300 GERMAN PARATROOPERS TO SEIZE IMPORTANT CROSSROADS IN THE NORTH.

CAPTURING THE NORTHERN AREA OF ANTWERP, BELGIUM, WOULD WEAKEN THE U.S. ARMY'S SUPPLY ROUTES AND PROVIDE THE GERMANS WITH VALUABLE SUPPLIES.

GERMAN COLONEL FRIEDRICH VON DER HEYDTE LED THE OPERATION, CODE-NAMED STOESSER. HE MADE HIS JUMP WITH A BROKEN ARM.

HIGH WINDS AND A BLINDING SNOWSTORM RESULTED IN ONLY 300 PARATROOPERS REACHING THE FINAL CROSSROAD LOCATION.

WITH SO FEW MEN, VON DER HEYDTE ABANDONED PLANS TO TAKE THE CROSSROADS. INSTEAD, HE ORGANIZED A GROUP OF SOLDIERS TO HARASS ALLIED TROOPS.

DESPITE BEING IN GREAT PAIN, VON DER HEYDTE USED HIS EXPERIENCE AS AN AIRBORNE COMMANDER TO SET UP AMBUSHES ALONG IMPORTANT ROADS AND JUNCTIONS.

DECEMBER 17, 1944. AS THE WORD SPREAD THAT A MAJOR ATTACK WAS HAPPENING, THE GERMANS LAUNCHED A SUPPORTING ATTACK CALLED OPERATION GREIF.

ABOUT 24 GERMANS WHO SPOKE ENGLISH SNEAKED INTO THE ALLIED AREA, WEARING U.S. UNIFORMS.

THIS OPERATION WAS LED BY COLONEL OTTO SKORZENY, LATER CALLED BY MANY, BOTH AXIS AND ALLIED, "THE MOST DANGEROUS MAN IN EUROPE."

THEY SPREAD CONFUSION BY MISDIRECTING U.S. TROOPS AND ATTEMPTING TO HOLD BRIDGES FOR THE GERMANS.

YOU'RE GOING THE WRONG WAY. ST. VITH IS TEN MILES WEST OF HERE!

RUMORS QUICKLY SPREAD THROUGHOUT U.S. FORCES IN THE REGION.

THEY'VE SNUCK IN THOUSANDS OF GERMANS IN EVERY UNIT OF OURS IN EUROPE!

YEAH, I HEARD THE GENERAL MIGHT REALLY BE A GERMAN IN DISGUISE!

TO IDENTIFY THE DISGUISED GERMAN COMMANDOS, U.S. SOLDIERS ASKED QUESTIONS THAT ONLY AMERICANS COULD ANSWER, LIKE THE NAME OF MICKEY MOUSE'S GIRLFRIEND, THE WORLD SERIES WINNER, OR THE CAPITAL OF ILLINOIS.

THESE QUESTIONS LED TO THE BRIEF DETENTION OF GENERAL OMAR BRADLEY, WHEN A GI INSISTED THAT THE CAPITAL OF ILLINOIS WAS CHICAGO.

YOU'RE WRONG, GENERAL!

BUT THE CAPITAL OF ILLINOIS REALLY *IS* SPRINGFIELD!

DESPITE THE EARLY PANIC CREATED BY SKORZENY'S COMMANDOS, THE INCREASED SECURITY LED TO THE CAPTURE OF SOME OF HIS MEN.

SKORZENY ESCAPED, BUT SOME OF HIS MEN MET THEIR END FROM A FIRING SQUAD. STILL, THE EFFECT OF OPERATION GREIF HURT AMERICAN MORALE FAR BEYOND THE ACTUAL MILITARY CONTRIBUTION TO THE BATTLE.

NEAR THE TOWN OF MALMEDY, BELGIUM, GERMAN SS COLONEL JOCHEN PEIPER CAPTURED ABOUT 120 AMERICAN SOLDIERS HEADING SOUTH.

AS PEIPER MOVED AHEAD, HIS SS OFFICERS ORDERED THE AMERICANS TO MARCH INTO AN OPEN FIELD.

MOVE IT! NOW!

SUDDENLY, THE GERMANS OPENED FIRE ON THE UNARMED AMERICANS.

THE AMERICANS TRIED TO ESCAPE INTO THE WOODS, BUT 86 WERE KILLED.

FROM THE AMERICAN POINT OF VIEW, THE MASSACRE AT MALMEDY IS THE MOST INFAMOUS EVENT OF THE BATTLE OF THE BULGE. ONE AMERICAN SURVIVOR WROTE, "IT TAKES A LONG TIME TO KILL 100 MEN, EVEN WHEN YOU USE MACHINE GUNS."

DECEMBER 18–19, 1944. PUSHING AHEAD TOWARD THE BELGIAN TOWN OF STAVELOT, PEIPER HOPED TO CAPTURE ALLIED FUEL SUPPLIES.

HE ENCOUNTERED STIFF RESISTANCE AND WAS FORCED TO TURN BACK WHEN U.S. ENGINEERS DESTROYED THE ONLY BRIDGE LEADING INTO THE TOWN.

ACROSS THE ENTIRE 80-MILE FRONT, THE GERMAN TIMETABLE FOR SUCCESS WAS SLOWED DUE TO THE TREMENDOUS COURAGE AND SKILL OF THE AMERICANS AT EVERY ROAD OR FIELD.

DECEMBER 16. U.S. PRIVATE FIRST CLASS HARRY ARVANNIS GRABBED A MORTAR WITH A MISSING BASE PLATE AND FIRED 30 ROUNDS AT THE GERMANS BY HAND, HOLDING THE TUBE BETWEEN HIS KNEES.

SEEING THAT ARVANNIS WAS OUT OF MORTAR ROUNDS, THE REMAINING GERMANS PUT BAYONETS ON THEIR RIFLES AND CHARGED HIS POSITION.

WITH ONLY HIS PISTOL REMAINING, PFC ARVANNIS FIRED UNTIL IT WAS EMPTY. HE KILLED THREE OF THE FOUR ATTACKING GERMANS.

OUT OF BULLETS, ARVANNIS THREW HIS 4-POUND REVOLVER AT THE LAST GERMAN, HITTING HIM ON THE FOREHEAD AND KILLING HIM INSTANTLY.

MORE AND MORE, EISENHOWER SAW THE IMPORTANCE OF THE SMALL BELGIAN TOWN OF BASTOGNE AND ITS CROSSROADS.

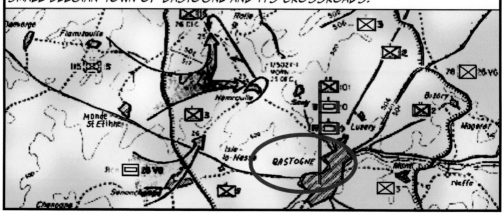

EISENHOWER KNEW THE GERMANS WOULD NEED BASTOGNE TO KEEP THEIR SUPPLY LINES OPEN EAST TO WEST.

EISENHOWER ORDERED GENERAL ANTHONY McAULIFFE AND THE 101ST AIRBORNE DIVISION TO MOVE INTO BASTOGNE IMMEDIATELY.

DECEMBER 19. GENERAL McAULIFFE AND HIS TROOPERS ARRIVED IN BASTOGNE MERE HOURS BEFORE THE GERMANS.

DECEMBER 16. CAPTAIN LEE BERWICK'S UNIT WAS OUT OF AMMUNITION WHEN HE SAW ABOUT 100 GERMANS COMING TOWARD HIM.

WE'VE GOT NOTHING LEFT, SIR! ALL WE CAN HIT THEM WITH NOW IS SNOWBALLS!

BERWICK DECIDED TO FOOL THE GERMANS INTO BELIEVING THEY HAD WALKED INTO A TRAP.

STANDING FACE-TO-FACE WITH THE ENEMY, BERWICK WARNED THAT A "MASSIVE ATTACK FORCE" WAS WAITING TO KILL THEM IF THEY DID NOT SURRENDER IMMEDIATELY.

PUT DOWN YOUR WEAPONS, NOW!

THE GERMANS BELIEVED BERWICK. HE CAPTURED 102 SOLDIERS AND TWO OFFICERS, TAKING THEIR WEAPONS TO CONTINUE THE FIGHT!

23

GENERAL EISENHOWER WAS THE ONLY AMERICAN OFFICER WHO SAW SOMETHING POSITIVE ABOUT THE GERMAN OFFENSIVE.

HE KNEW IT WOULD BE DIFFICULT TO FIGHT THE GERMANS IN THEIR WELL-PREPARED DEFENSIVE POSITIONS.

HE ALSO KNEW THAT BY ATTACKING ALLIED POSITIONS, THE GERMANS WOULD EXPOSE THEMSELVES TO COUNTERATTACK.

BY RUSHING OUT FROM HIS FIXED DEFENSES, THE ENEMY GIVES US THE CHANCE TO TURN HIS GAMBLE INTO HIS WORST DEFEAT.

FORWARD OUTPOST OF THE 101ST AIRBORNE, BASTOGNE.

AS GENERAL EISENHOWER MET WITH HIS STAFF IN FRANCE, THE GERMANS SURROUNDED BASTOGNE AND PREPARED TO TAKE IT BY FORCE.

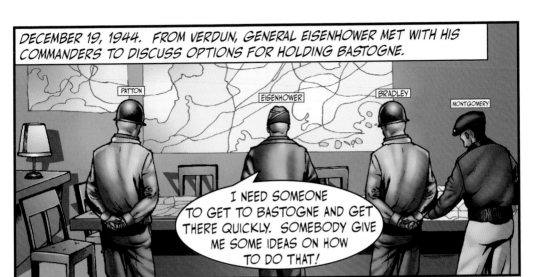

DECEMBER 19, 1944. FROM VERDUN, GENERAL EISENHOWER MET WITH HIS COMMANDERS TO DISCUSS OPTIONS FOR HOLDING BASTOGNE.

PATTON EISENHOWER BRADLEY MONTGOMERY

I NEED SOMEONE TO GET TO BASTOGNE AND GET THERE QUICKLY. SOMEBODY GIVE ME SOME IDEAS ON HOW TO DO THAT!

I CAN ATTACK INTO BASTOGNE WITH THREE DIVISIONS IN LESS THAN 72 HOURS.

BE SERIOUS, GEORGE! YOUR 3RD ARMY IS MORE THAN 125 MILES TO THE SOUTH!

IMPOSSIBLE! YOU'D HAVE TO STOP YOUR OFFENSIVE IN THE SOUTH AND COMPLETELY CHANGE THE 3RD ARMY'S DIRECTION NORTH!

I ORDERED MY STAFF TO BEGIN PLANNING A BASTOGNE OPERATION TWO DAYS AGO. MY LEAD UNITS ARE ALREADY ON THE MOVE. . .UNLESS YOU WANT ME TO PULL THEM BACK!

THE JOB IS YOURS, GEORGE. GET TO BASTOGNE IMMEDIATELY. LET'S PRAY OUR BOYS CAN HOLD ON IN THE MEANTIME.

25

DECEMBER 19, 1944. MAJOR ARTHUR C. PARKER PREPARED TO STOP THE GERMAN ADVANCE AT A CROSSROADS ALONG THE NORTHERN BOUNDARY.

WITH MOST OF HIS UNIT DEAD OR CAPTURED, PARKER GATHERED ALL THE MEN AND EQUIPMENT HE COULD FIND AND TOOK CHARGE.

KNOWING THAT THE GERMANS WOULD ATTACK WITH OVERWHELMING FORCE, PARKER PREPARED AN "ALAMO DEFENSE"—TO FIGHT UNTIL THE LAST MAN WAS DEAD.

PARKER KNEW THAT THE BARAQUE DE FRAITURE CROSSROADS LAY AT A CRITICAL POINT.

THE GERMANS COULD MOVE IN EITHER DIRECTION TO SURROUND OR PENETRATE THE ALLIED FRONT LINE.

PARKER REFUSED TO RETREAT EVEN THOUGH HE WAS SURROUNDED AND UNDER INTENSE FIRE FROM ALL SIDES.

SERIOUSLY WOUNDED BY MORTAR FRAGMENTS, PARKER'S SACRIFICE WAS NOT IN VAIN.

HIS OUTNUMBERED UNIT HELD FOR TWO DAYS AND SERIOUSLY HAMPERED THE GERMAN ATTACK TIMETABLE.

FARTHER SOUTH, LIEUTENANT ERIC F. WOOD, SURROUNDED AND CAPTURED BY GERMAN INFANTRY, MADE A MAD DASH FOR THE SAFETY OF THE FOREST.

SUCCESSFULLY REACHING THE FOREST, WOOD HID FROM THE GERMANS AND KEPT MELTING DEEPER AND DEEPER INTO THE THICK FOREST.

GIVEN FOOD AND SHELTER BY SEVERAL BELGIAN FAMILIES, WOOD GATHERED INFORMATION ABOUT NAZI POSITIONS IN THE AREA, AND HE DEVELOPED A PLAN.

THE COUNTRYSIDE IS FULL OF GERMANS!

I'LL FIGHT MY WAY BACK TO MY OUTFIT AND START A WAR OF MY OWN!

OVER THE NEXT THREE WEEKS, WOOD WAGED A PRIVATE WAR ON THE GERMANS. HE BECAME A LEGEND TO THE LOCAL BELGIAN PEOPLE.

FINALLY CORNERED AND OVERRUN, WOOD KILLED SEVEN GERMANS WITH HIS LAST SEVEN BULLETS BEFORE DYING FROM MULTIPLE GUNSHOT WOUNDS.

MEANWHILE, ANOTHER BRAVE SOLDIER, CORPORAL HENRY WARNER, WAS REFUSING TO RETREAT FROM HIS OVERRUN POSITION.

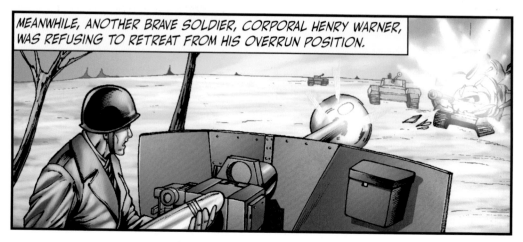

OUT OF ANTITANK AMMUNITION, WARNER ATTACKED A THIRD TANK WITH HIS PISTOL, KILLING THE TANK COMMANDER IN A PISTOL DUEL.

WITH ONLY HIS PISTOL, WARNER FORCED THE TANK TO RETREAT.

THE NEXT DAY CORPORAL WARNER WAS KILLED IN BATTLE. HE WAS ONE OF 17 AMERICANS TO BE AWARDED THE CONGRESSIONAL MEDAL OF HONOR FOR ACTIONS DURING THE BATTLE OF THE BULGE.

THE MAIN GERMAN ATTACK TO THE NORTH WAS HOPELESSLY STALLED BY THE AMERICANS. THEY JUST WOULD NOT GIVE UP.

PULL YOUR TANK BEHIND ME, BUDDY! I'M THE 82ND AIRBORNE AND THIS IS AS FAR AS THE NAZIS ARE GOING!

PFC MARTIN OF THE FAMOUS 82ND AIRBORNE "ALL-AMERICAN" DIVISION CAUGHT THE SPIRIT OF U.S. RESISTANCE ACROSS THE BATTLEFIELD.

GENERAL BRUCE CLARKE FINALLY PULLED BACK FROM A HEROIC SEVEN-DAY STAND IN THE SMALL TOWN OF ST. VITH.

THE SUCCESSFUL STAND OF THE INEXPERIENCED 106TH INFANTRY AT ST. VITH PLAYED A HUGE ROLE IN DESTROYING THE GERMAN PLANS NEEDED FOR SUCCESS.

DECEMBER 21, 1944. UNITS IN THE NORTH BEGIN REPORTING "ALL QUIET" AS THE MAIN GERMAN ATTACK MOVES SOUTHWEST. THIS MOVEMENT CREATED THE "BULGE" IN THE LINE THAT GAVE THE BATTLE ITS NAME.

THE NAZI DO-OR-DIE OFFENSIVE WAS HOPELESSLY OFF SCHEDULE.

WE HAVE RUN OUT OF TIME.

WE MUST ONLY HOPE THAT ATTACKS IN THE SOUTH HAVE BEEN MORE SUCCESSFUL.

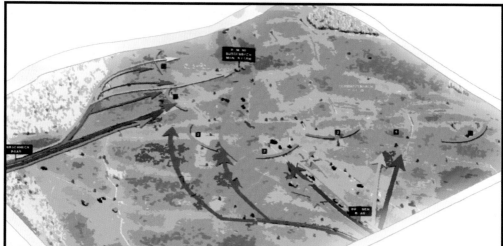

BY THE MORNING OF DECEMBER 21, HEROIC STANDS BY AMERICAN SOLDIERS HAD STALLED THE GERMAN ADVANCE ACROSS THE ENTIRE LINE.

DECEMBER 22, 1944. AS THE BATTLE RAGED ACROSS BELGIUM AND LUXEMBOURG, ALL EYES TURNED TO THE LITTLE VILLAGE OF BASTOGNE.

DON'T SHOOT! WE HAVE A MESSAGE FOR YOUR COMMANDING OFFICER!

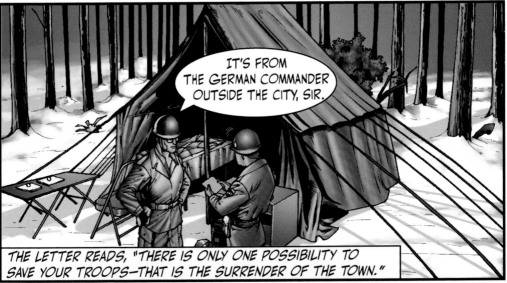

IT'S FROM THE GERMAN COMMANDER OUTSIDE THE CITY, SIR.

THE LETTER READS, "THERE IS ONLY ONE POSSIBILITY TO SAVE YOUR TROOPS—THAT IS THE SURRENDER OF THE TOWN."

WHAT SHOULD I TELL HIM, SIR?

31

COLONEL HARPER DELIVERED GENERAL McAULIFFE'S WRITTEN RESPONSE BACK TO THE GERMANS.

I DO NOT UNDERSTAND. WHAT IS THE MEANING OF "NUTS!"?

IN PLAIN ENGLISH, "NUTS" MEANS GO TO HELL! AND IF YOU CONTINUE TO ATTACK, WE WILL KILL EVERY GERMAN WHO TRIES TO BREAK INTO THE CITY!

EVEN GENERAL PATTON, MANY MILES AWAY, HEARD OF GENERAL McAULIFFE'S "NUTS" REPLY.

A MAN SO ELOQUENT MUST NOT BE ALLOWED TO PERISH.

MEANWHILE AROUND BASTOGNE, CAPTURED AMERICAN SOLDIERS PREPARED FOR THE COMING OF THE DAWN AND WHAT COULD VERY WELL BE THEIR LAST DAY ON EARTH.

DECEMBER 23, 1944. AS LEAD ELEMENTS OF PATTON'S 3RD ARMY ATTACK THE GERMANS OUTSIDE BASTOGNE, HIS CHAPLAIN OFFERS A PRAYER.

" . . . AND WE HUMBLY BESEECH THEE TO RESTRAIN THESE RAINS. GRANT US FAIR WEATHER FOR BATTLE."

"HEARKEN TO US WHO CALL UPON THEE THAT WE MAY ADVANCE TO VICTORY, CRUSH OUR ENEMIES, AND ESTABLISH JUSTICE AMONG NATIONS."

THE SKIES CLEARED. ALLIED AIRCRAFT, GROUNDED DUE TO BAD WEATHER FOR THE LAST WEEK, NOW FILLED THE SKIES.

THE AMERICAN SOLDIERS RECEIVED MUCH-NEEDED FOOD, AMMUNITION, AND MEDICAL SUPPLIES.

ANY HOPE THE GERMANS HELD OF TAKING BASTOGNE WENT UP IN THE SMOKE OF THEIR BURNING TANKS AND ARTILLERY.

OUTSIDE BASTOGNE, PRIVATE MAX CAIN WAS ONE OF THE EXHAUSTED BUT MOTIVATED THIRD ARMY SOLDIERS SPOTTING FOR THE ARTILLERY AND DODGING GERMANS AT EVERY TURN.

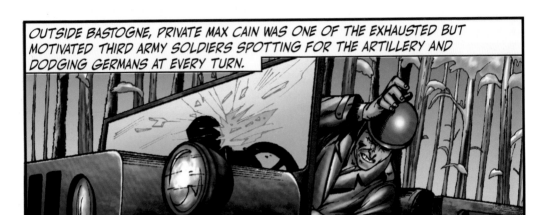

HIT BY SNIPER FIRE AND DRIVING THROUGH AN ARTILLERY BARRAGE, CAIN LOST CONTROL OF HIS JEEP.

A GERMAN SOLDIER WATCHED, AND DID NOT FIRE. CAIN PULLED HIS INJURED LIEUTENANT FROM THE JEEP TOWARD THE SAFETY OF A DITCH.

PRIVATE CAIN WONDERED YEARS LATER IF THE GERMAN SOLDIER MADE IT SAFELY HOME AND WAS THANKFUL FOR HAVING SURVIVED THAT DAY.

ACROSS THE ALLIED FRONT, GENERAL EISENHOWER OFFERED A HISTORIC APPROACH TO GETTING FRESH TROOPS TO FORWARD DEPLOYED UNITS.

AFRICAN AMERICAN SOLDIERS, ASSIGNED TO OTHER SERVICE UNITS, WERE GIVEN THE OPPORTUNITY TO VOLUNTEER FOR COMBAT DUTY WITH THE INFANTRY.

MORE THAN 3,500 SOLDIERS RESPONDED, MANY TAKING REDUCTIONS IN RANK TO JOIN THE FIGHT. THE OUTSTANDING BATTLE ACHIEVEMENTS OF THESE VOLUNTEERS HELPED PAVE THE WAY FOR THE RACIAL INTEGRATION OF THE U.S. ARMY.

AMERICAN SOLDIERS OF MANY BACKGROUNDS PLAYED AN IMPORTANT PART IN DEFEATING THE GERMANS.

CHRISTMAS DAY, 1944. HEAVY SNOWS BROUGHT A SLIGHT PAUSE TO THE BATTLE AS THE SURROUNDING HILLS OF BASTOGNE WERE AT FIRST STRANGELY QUIET.

DO YOU HEAR THAT?

I DON'T HEAR ANYTHING.

THAT'S MY POINT. IT'S SO QUIET, YOU CAN ALMOST FEEL SOMETHING BIG IS ABOUT TO . . . HEY! DID YOU HEAR THAT?

THAT WAS NO GERMAN TIGER! THAT WAS A U.S. SHERMAN TANK!

WHAT DOES THAT MEAN, JOE?

IT MEANS THAT THIS IS MY BEST CHRISTMAS EVER, SAM!

DECEMBER 26, 1944. AFTER SIX DAYS OF INTENSE FIGHTING, THE THIRD ARMY LINKED UP WITH THE 101ST AIRBORNE AT BASTOGNE.

CHRISTMAS MAY HAVE COME A DAY LATE FOR THE ALLIES, BUT IT DELIVERED A CELEBRATION THE SOLDIERS AND CITIZENS OF BASTOGNE WOULD NEVER FORGET.

HOW ARE YOU, GENERAL?

GEE, I'M MIGHTY GLAD TO SEE YOU!

THE SIEGE OF BASTOGNE WAS OVER.

FROM DECEMBER 27, 1944, THROUGH JANUARY 7, 1945, THE ALLIES ATTACKED TO TAKE BACK THE GROUND THEY LOST SINCE DECEMBER 16.

FROM THE NORTH, FIELD MARSHAL MONTGOMERY ATTACKED ON JANUARY 3, TRAPPING THE GERMANS BETWEEN THE BRITISH AND U.S. ARMIES.

SOME GERMAN UNITS TRIED TO HOLD THEIR GROUND BUT THEY WERE COMPLETELY WIPED OUT.

AAARGH!

AS THE FIGHTING WOUND DOWN, GENERAL BRADLEY, 12TH ARMY GROUP COMMANDER, WROTE:

"OUR ASSESSMENT OF THE ENEMY INTENT TO LAUNCH A MAJOR ATTACK WAS WRONG, BUT OUR ESTIMATE OF HIS CAPABILITIES WAS CORRECT."

AFTER ENLARGING THE ATTACK ROUTES AROUND BASTOGNE, U.S. AND BRITISH TROOPS ATTACKED TO ELIMINATE THE "BULGE" IN THE LINE.

HITLER FINALLY GAVE THE ORDER TO WITHDRAW ON JANUARY 7, 1945.

BY JANUARY 30, THE ALLIES HAD ELIMINATED ALL THE GAINS MADE BY THE GERMANS DURING THE ENTIRE ARDENNES CAMPAIGN.

FROM HIS HEADQUARTERS IN HESSEN, HITLER REALIZED THAT HE WOULD SOON FIND HIMSELF AT THE MERCY OF HIS ENEMIES.

IN LESS THAN 30 DAYS OF FIGHTING, 16,000 GERMAN SOLDIERS WERE KILLED AND ANOTHER 41,600 WERE WOUNDED.

DEFEATED, PEIPER MADE HIS WAY THROUGH ALLIED LINES BACK TO GERMANY. ALTHOUGH HE SURVIVED, HE LEFT HIS TANKS BEHIND.

MOST OF MY FRIENDS ARE GONE NOW. THEY ARE WAITING FOR ME TO JOIN THEM IN VALHALLA.*

*IN NORSE MYTHOLOGY, VALHALLA WAS A HALL IN WHICH THE GOD ODIN WELCOMED THE SOULS OF KILLED HEROES.

THE LOSS ON THE ALLIED SIDE WAS EQUALLY FEARSOME: MORE THAN 19,000 DEAD AND 47,493 WOUNDED. BUT WHILE THE ALLIES COULD RECOVER, THE GERMANS COULD NOT. THEY JUST DID NOT HAVE ENOUGH MEN OR RESOURCES LEFT.

AFTER THE WAR, REICH MINISTER OF ARMS ALBERT SPEER PUBLISHED A BEST-SELLING BOOK, INSIDE THE THIRD REICH.

THE FAILURE OF THE ARDENNES OFFENSIVE MEANS THE WAR IS OVER.

THE WORD SPREAD QUICKLY THROUGHOUT GERMANY THAT THE WAR WAS LOST.

AS THE ARDENNES OFFENSIVE FAILED, THE MUCH-DREADED INVASION FROM RUSSIA WAS UNDERWAY.

NO LONGER STRONG AND CONFIDENT, HITLER ABANDONED HIS EAGLE'S NEST FORTRESS AND TOOK REFUGE IN HIS BERLIN BUNKER. HE WOULD NEVER LEAVE ALIVE.

FROM HUNGARY TO CZECHOSLOVAKIA TO THE GERMAN BORDER, THE RUSSIAN ARMY MARCHED ACROSS EASTERN EUROPE.

HITLER'S THIRD REICH, DESTINED TO LAST 1,000 YEARS, DIED AT THE AGE OF 12.

GENERAL PATTON WAS KILLED IN A CAR ACCIDENT IN 1945 AND IS BURIED WITH 5,000 FELLOW BULGE HEROES IN HAMM, LUXEMBOURG.

HE BECAME AN IMPORTANT AMERICAN SYMBOL OF MILITARY COURAGE. THE 1970 MOVIE OF HIS LIFE WON MANY ACADEMY AWARDS.

PATTON: A Salute to a Rebel

IN THE BELGIAN FOREST WHERE LIEUTENANT ERIC WOOD DIED, A SMALL MONUMENT READS, "ERIC FISHER WOOD, U.S. ARMY, FOUND A HERO'S DEATH AFTER UNSPARING SINGLE-HANDED COMBAT."

HE WAS THE ONLY AMERICAN IN WORLD WAR II TO RECEIVE THE CROSS OF CHEVALIER OF THE BELGIAN ORDER OF LEOPOLD I WITH GOLD PALM, BELGIUM'S HIGHEST AWARD.

MAJOR ARTHUR PARKER SURVIVED HIS WOUNDS AND RETURNED TO TAKE COMMAND OF THE 589TH ARTILLERY BATTALION.

YEARS LATER, GENERAL JAMES GAVIN, COMMANDER OF THE 82ND AIRBORNE DIVISION DURING THE BATTLE, WROTE THAT PARKER'S STAND "WAS ONE OF THE GREATEST ACTIONS OF THE WAR."

THE CITY OF BASTOGNE NAMED ITS TOWN CENTER McAULIFFE SQUARE. GENERAL McAULIFFE IS CELEBRATED EVERY YEAR ON THE ANNIVERSARY OF HIS LEGENDARY "NUTS" REPLY.

MAX CAIN RETURNED HOME IN 1946. THE MONEY HE SENT HOME WHILE AT WAR SAVED THE LIFE OF HIS STARVING FAMILY.

HE WAS AWARDED THE BRONZE STAR FOR HIS ACTIONS IN THE ARDENNES AND DIED IN 1984.

THE LUXEMBOURG AMERICAN CEMETERY AND MEMORIAL IN HAMM PROVIDES THE FINAL RESTING PLACE FOR OVER 5,000 AMERICANS WHO DIED DURING THE BATTLE OF THE BULGE.

THE END

AFTER THE BATTLE

The great German offensive had been defeated, although it was not until the end of January that the Allies were able to recapture all the areas that had been taken. By that time the war had moved on, and the Germans launched another smaller offensive in Alsace (code-named Operation Nordwind) that never achieved its objectives. On January 12, 1945, the Soviet Union began its great offensive in the east, in which the Russians drove deep into Poland and German-occupied East Prussia. The eastern and western Allies were now closing in on the German heartland.

The Battle of the Bulge had bled the German army dry on the western front, and it was now hard-pressed to prevent the Allies from crossing the River Rhine, the traditional western frontier of Germany. The Germans had lost almost 100,000 men in the campaign and almost all their remaining force of tanks. For their part, the Americans lost about 80,000 men, enough to weaken their army but not to prevent them

from launching their own offensive.

In early February 1945, the British and the Americans attacked all along the western front. Montgomery crossed the Rhine north of Germany's industrial region of the Ruhr, while Hodges and Patton launched attacks farther to the south. The Americans pushed the Germans

George S. Patton awarded the Distinguished Service Cross to Brigadier General Anthony McAuliffe for his bravery at Bastogne.

German troops withdrew on Hitler's orders when he knew the battle was lost. The Americans began a slow but steady advance.

back to the Rhine and then swept across it after capturing a bridge at Remagen. If the Germans had remained on the defensive in December 1945, they would probably have had the troops to delay the Allies. However, concentrating all their best troops and launching them into the attack in the Ardennes meant that once they had been defeated the Germans had no troops left to plug the gap.

If the Germans had won the Battle of the Bulge, they might have been able to defeat the western Allies and force them to sign a humiliating peace treaty. However, the Germans probably overestimated their own ability and underestimated the abilities of the Americans. They also did not understand the Allied commitment to win, regardless of the cost. Above all, the Allied victory in the Battle of the Bulge meant that the Germans were now unable to stop the Soviet Red Army or the western Allies from sweeping into Germany, and the war would now be over by the end of April 1945. In the end, the great German offensive designed to salvage a victory in Europe only managed to hasten the collapse of Germany, bringing an end to the evil Nazi regime, which had plunged the world into war.

GLOSSARY

allies People or countries that give support to each other.

ammunition Explosives, such as bullets, that are fired from weapons.

artillery Large, heavy guns that are mounted on wheels or tracks.

assessment An evaluation about something or a situation.

bulge A swollen part of something.

deployed To have been spread out in battle in a specific formation.

fortress A place that is strengthened against attack.

fuehrer German for leader. Adolf Hitler used this title.

fuel depot A place for storing fuel.

howitzer A cannon with a short barrel that is used for firing at high angles.

infantry The branch of an army trained to fight on foot.

integration The act of incorporating people as equals in society.

mortar rounds Shots fired from weapons.

mythology A popular belief about someone or something.

panzer A German tank used during World War II.

paratrooper A member of troops that are trained to jump from an airplane.

patriotic Loving one's country and supporting everything it stands for.

PFC Private first class. The rank of a person in the army that is above a private and below a corporal.

regime A form of government.

resistance The act of fighting back.

siege A military attack on a city in order to force it to surrender.

stand A fight of resistance

telegraph A device for sending messages over long distances.

Third Reich The name for Germany used by the Nazis during the years from January 1933 to April 1945.

treaty A formal agreement between two or more countries.

Wehrmacht German armed forces; the unified forces of the army, navy, and air force.

FOR MORE INFORMATION

ORGANIZATIONS

Veterans of the Battle of the Bulge
P.O. Box 101418
Arlington, VA 22210-4418
(703) 528-4058
Web site: http://www.battleofthebulge.org

World War II Federation, Inc.
P.O. Box 711
Waynesburg, PA 15370-0711
(724) 627 8545
Web site: http://www.wwiifederation.org

FOR FURTHER READING

Cain, Bill. *Hitler's Last Gamble: Battle of the Bulge* (Graphic History). New York: Osprey Publishing, 2007.

Jordan, David. *Battle of the Bulge*. Osceola, WI: Motorbooks International, 2003.

Kershaw, Alex. *The Longest Winter: The Battle of the Bulge and the Epic Story of WWII's Most Decorated Platoon*. New York: Da Capo Press, 2004.

McNeese, Tim. *Battle of the Bulge* (Great Battles Through the Ages). New York: Chelsea House Publications, 2003.

Neill, George W. *Infantry Soldier: Holding the Line at the Battle of the Bulge*. Norman, OK: University of Oklahoma Press, 2002.

Sears, Stephen W. *The Battle of the Bulge*. IBooks, Inc., 2005.

Toland, John. *Battle: The Story of the Bulge*. Lincoln, NE: Bison Books, 1999.

Zaloga, Steven J. *Battle of the Bulge 1944: Campaign 115: (1)*. New York: Osprey Publishing, 2003.

Zaloga, Steven J. *Battle of the Bulge 1944: Campaign 145: (2)*. New York: Osprey Publishing, 2004.

INDEX

WEB SITES

Due to the changing nature of Internet links, the Rosen Publishing Group, Inc. has developed an online list of Web sites related to the subject of this book. This site is updated regularly. Please use this link to access the list:

http://www.rosenlinks.com/gbwwt/babu